# Victorian Dreams

## The Creative Art of
## Lace Making by Machine

## Jenny Haskins

# Contents

EDITORIAL
Managing Editor: Judy Poulos
Editorial Assistant: Ella Martin
Editorial Coordinator: Margaret Kelly

PHOTOGRAPHY
Andy Payne

ILLUSTRATIONS
Pattern Sheet: Lesley Griffith
Additional Illustrations: Jenny Haskins

STYLING
Louise Owens

DESIGN AND PRODUCTION
Manager: Sheridan Carter
Design: Lulu Dougherty
Layout and Finished Art: Gavin Murrell
and Stephen Joseph

VICTORIAN DREAMS ISBN 1 86343 126 8

Published by J.B. Fairfax Press Pty Limited
80-82 McLachlan Avenue, Rushcutters Bay 2011 Australia
Ph: (02) 361 6366  Fax: (02) 360 6262
Printed by Toppan Printing Co, Hong Kong

DISTRIBUTION AND SALES
Sales Enquiries: J.B. Fairfax Press Pty Limited
Tel: (02) 361 6366 Fax: (02) 360 6262
Newsagents Direct Distribution and
Storewide Magazine Distributors
Tel: (02) 353 9911 Fax: (02) 669 2305

PHOTOGRAPHY CREDITS

All the fresh flowers and the pearl and rosebud necklace from
Lisa Milasas (02) 524 8918

Tassel on the fan from Kim Lauren Exclusives (02) 427 5147

Antique silver pieces from Gwenda's Antiques (02) 327 8840

Ribbons from Offray Ribbons (02) 649 2777

Background fabric from Carrington Fabrics  (02) 699 9533

# Dedication

Any talents, expertise or creative ability that I may have are direct gifts from
God. I have no formal training but, as in the parable of the talents,
I have worked and shared these gifts and been blessed.
Nothing comes about through the efforts of one person; many people
contribute. Thank you to those who have always been there for me –
particularly my beautiful family – my husband, Laurie; my children, Jason,
Simon and Samantha; all my students, from whom I learned more than I
taught; and my boss, who encouraged me in the spirit of this poem.

*'Come to the edge,' he said.*

*And I was afraid.*

*'Come to the edge,' he said.*

*And I was afraid.*

*'Come to the edge,' he said.*

*And I came to the edge.*

*He pushed me … and I flew.*

I also want to give mention to the generous people who have provided the
wonderful products used in this book and to tell you how to contact them.

In Australia
Needlecraft International Pty Limited
  (tulle and laces)
  96 Rowe St, Eastwood, NSW 2122
  Toll free 008 263 977
Helmar Pty Limited (Helmar products)
  37/8 Victoria Ave, Victoria Park
  Castle Hill, NSW 2154
  (02) 899 2666

In the United States
Capitol Imports Inc (tulle and laces)
  2518 Cathay Court, Tallahassee
  Florida 32317
  Toll free 1-800 521-7647
Sullivans (Helmar products)
  224 William St, Bensonville
  Illinois 60106
  Toll free 1-800 862-8586

# Introduction

I cannot remember a time in my life when I was not using my hands in some creative way, whether it be with a paint brush, a needle, a pencil or a knitting needle. Channelling my boundless energy into these creative activities probably kept me out of a lot of mischief.

My mother taught me all the basic hand-embroidery stitches and I took off. I still have some of the pieces I did as a child. I knitted my first jumper when I was seven and have made dolls clothes for as long as I can remember.

Even though I did well at both art and sewing at school, these talents were set aside until I was married and decorating my home became an important part of my life. Financially, I did not have the means to achieve my expectations but, as necessity is the mother of invention, off to technical college I went to do a course in soft furnishings. After making all my own soft furnishings, I turned to family and friends to fill my creative needs.

This led to many more courses while my family was small. I was introduced to porcelain painting, which I took up with a passion, and was soon teaching all over Australia, with my work being published in several books.

There soon followed fabric and silk painting and folk art. When needlework came back into fashion with grub roses, lazy daisies and silk ribbon embroidery – all of which I had been doing for years – the artistic and design skills which I had learned over the years allowed me to draw my own designs. These were soon picked up by craft and women's magazines. All the designs and Victoriana illustrations in this book are my own originals.

The publicity led me to my present position which was a total departure because, even though I made a lot of my own clothes, I had no formal training in sewing.

When I was first introduced to the Pfaff Creative 1475 CD, I could not believe that it had never been exploited to any degree. Here was a magic machine which could re-create the beauty of a bygone era using the technology of today. The wonder of computer technology introduced the possibility of creating not only new designs, using the stitches built into the machine, but of designing my own stitches and then sending them to the machine to stitch them out.

This book is the result of this adventure of discovery that began when I was a small child. I would also like to think that the book challenges and inspires the reader, perhaps reaching out to someone who is creative but afraid to 'give it a go'.

These days – still juggling the demands of motherhood and a career – I am employed full-time as the National Education and Training Manager for Pfaff Australia and New Zealand, where I am responsible for training consultants and dealers; writing and planning classes; setting up craft shows; coordinating and designing samples, fashion parades, editorial and media promotions; and teaching all over the world.

*Jenny*

# Techniques

## FABRIC PREPARATION

Good preparation of fabric will ensure a result you will be proud of.

If you are unsure of the characteristics of the particular fabric you have purchased, begin by washing and ironing all the cotton net tulle. If you are sure of the quality of the fabric, such as that from Capitol Imports, pre-washing is not necessary.

Allow the tulle to dry somewhere out of the direct sun, then iron it flat. Cut out your patterns or the desired shape of the fabric before treating it with a liquid fabric stabiliser such as Helmar's Fabric Stiffener. Liquid fabric stabiliser washes out when the embroidery is completed.

If an entire pattern piece is to be embroidered, remember that the embroidery can alter the shape of the fabric. In this case, cut out the general shape of the pattern piece, cutting it bigger than you actually need. Complete all the embroidery before finally cutting out the piece to its exact shape.

Generally, it is not necessary to treat an entire piece with fabric stabiliser; treat only the area that is to be embroidered. Apply the fabric stabiliser with a paint brush or spray, following the manufacturer's instructions. You don't need to do all your stabilising in one go; do each area as you need to. Allow the tulle to dry somewhere out of the sun, then iron it flat.

If you do stabilise an entire pattern piece, make sure the tulle returns to the shape of the pattern when you are ironing it and that the grain is always straight.

## EMBROIDERY

Always do a test embroidery of any new pattern or stitch that you are going to do. This should be done in its entirety on a test piece of stabilised fabric to enable you to check not only the effectiveness of the embroidery, but the stiffness of the fabric as well.

Beginning on page 7, you will find a pict- orial directory of the embroidery stitches used in the book. These are meant to serve only as a guide. Your sewing machine may offer you a slightly different version of some stitches, which will give a very similar effect, or you might enjoy experimenting with your own sewing machine to see what different effects you can achieve.

## CUTTING AWAY

When the embroidery is completed, you will often be told to cut away the excess fabric on the edge of a piece. This cutting away will give you the look of a lace edge.

It is important to treat all areas to be cut away with a product that will stop the fabric fraying and the embroidery from unravelling. There are a number of these on the market, but the one I have used in this book is Helmar's Fray Stoppa. It is easy to apply and, once dry, allows you to cut very close to the stitching without the anxiety that nicking the stitches will cause the whole embroidery to unravel. Fray stoppers will not wash out.

## TRACING THE DESIGN

All the embroidery designs for the projects in this book are provided either on the Pattern Sheet or accompany the project instructions.

Tracing the design is easy to do as the tulle is transparent, making tracing paper unnecessary and allowing you to trace directly on to the fabric.

Place the tulle over your chosen design and then, using a blue wipe-off fabric marker pen, trace over the design.

You can iron over this marker pen design as it is drawn over the fabric stabiliser and will wash out in hot soapy water.

# Lacemaking Stitches

*There are many and varied scallop-edge and embroidery stitches on today's sophisticated sewing machines. Use the stitches shown here as a guide. If the particular stitch is not available on your sewing machine, choose a stitch that matches it as closely as possible. Don't be afraid to alter the width, length and density of the stitches to suit your pattern. This quite often gives an entirely fresh and delightful look to the stitch. Using your twin needle button also alters the width of your stitch.*

*Open scalloped edge*

*Stepped open scalloped edge*

*Filled-in scallop*

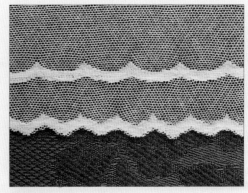

*Twin needle scallop*

*Stepped twin needle scallop*

*Shaped scallop*

*Stepped shaped scallop*

*Large scallop with smaller scallop around large scallop*

*Double-scalloped edge*

*Reduced-scalloped edge*

*Cutaway edge*

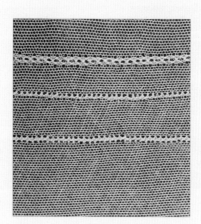

*Wing needle hem stitch*

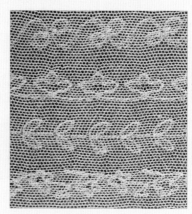

*Open embroidery stitch*

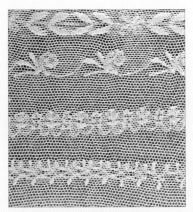

*Part open, part filled-in embroidery stitch*

*Freehand-look stitches*

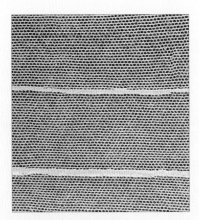

*Appliqué/satin stitch*

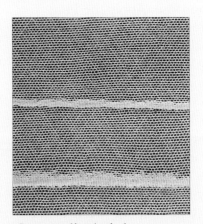

*Grass appliqué stitch*

*Closed or filled-in embroidery stitch*

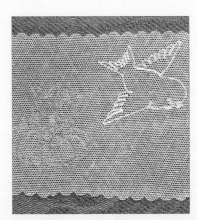

*Computer-designed stitches*

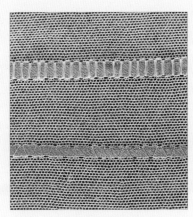

*Ribbon insertion stitch*

*Pulled-up ribbon insertion*

*Series of stitches to form lace with entredeux*

# Materials

### Blue Wipe-off Fabric Marker Pen

Also called water-fading or wash-out pens, these pens are essential for tracing the designs on to the fabric. Because they disappear completely when hot water is applied, you can be confident that any tracing lines that are not covered with stitching will wipe or wash away.

The transparent nature of the fabrics you will be working on allows you to trace a design directly on to the fabric with the blue pen without having to use tracing paper.

Ironing over the blue tracings will not make them permanent as they are drawn over fabric stabiliser which itself washes out.

### Embroidery Hoop

An embroidery hoop, with the inner ring bound, is occasionally required for machine-embroidery.

### Fabric

One hundred per cent natural fibre fabrics, such as fine cotton net tulle or voile are best. The finer the fabric is the better the result will be. The cotton net tulle used in the projects in this book is of exceptionally good quality and comes from Capitol Imports.

### Fabric Stabiliser

The use of fabric stabiliser before machine-embroidery eliminates the need for a hoop and holds your fabric firmly so that it does not bunch up. Fabric stabiliser washes out completely when the embroidery is completed.

There are many liquid, fabric and paper stabilisers on the market; the best for our purposes is a liquid fabric stabiliser such as Helmar's Fabric Stiffener. This can either be painted or sprayed on to the tulle. You may need to use several applications to achieve the necessary degree of stability.

When you have chosen the particular product you intend to use, follow the manufacturer's instructions for its application.

### Fray Stoppa

The delicate appearance of this method of embroidering lace, particularly on the lace edges, requires that the straight edges of fabric be cut away after embroidery to reveal the lace fabric or the lacy edge. To ensure that the fabric will not fray after it has been cut away, you will need to treat it with a fray stopper. Helmar's Fray Stoppa is an ideal product for this purpose. Apply the Fray Stoppa to all scalloped edges that are to be cut away. Allow the fabric to dry, then cut away the fabric with a pair of small sharp scissors, cutting as close as possible to the stitches.

### Lace Pins

It is important not to damage the delicate fabrics while you are working and to still have the benefit of pins that hold your work securely, ready for stitching. Using special lace pins will give you this 'holding' while at the same time protecting your delicate fabric. Choose pins with a glass head for ease of removal.

### Needles

A size 70 sewing machine needle is best for this type of work. Change your needle quite frequently as a blunt needle will tear the tulle. A 2.5/80 twin needle and a 120 wing needle are also used to produce a variety of stitches.

### Presser Foot

Choose an open-toed presser foot on your sewing machine as this will allow you to see your design as you sew.

### Scissors

Apart from your usual pair of dressmakers

scissors for cutting fabric, you will need a small pair of Fiskars or Pfaff scissors. Their sharp points cut neatly into tight corners and are the best for cutting away fabric from scallops and embroidery.

### Sewing Machine

Any top-of-the-range computerised sewing machine can be used for this type of lacemaking. The more stitches available on your machine, the more varied and interesting your results will be. The Pfaff Creative 1475 CD is ideal because it is the most versatile and allows more creative stitch possibilities.

Only with the Pfaff Creative 1475 CD computerised sewing machine, do you also have the possibility of designing on a PC (personal computer), transferring the design to your sewing machine's memory and then stitching out the design.

### Silk or Satin Ribbon

Many of the projects in this book are trimmed with bows and ribbons in the Victorian manner. Choose ribbons to complement your lace pieces.

### Tape Measure and Ruler

You will need to have handy a good metric and imperial tape measure with firm ends and a ruler for marking in the straight lines that will be your guidelines for embroidery.

### Thread

The denier of the thread you choose will depend on the density of the net. For finer tulle use Madeira Tanne 80; for a coarser net choose 30 to 40 denier thread. Always use one hundred per cent cotton thread.

### Vliesofix, Wonder Under or Stitch Witchery

This is a double-sided fusible web used for attaching motifs or appliqué pieces.

### Wire

Some of the projects will require you to use wire of various thicknesses to shape or support the lace; as in a flower petal or a butterfly's wing. The materials listing for each project will tell you which type of wire you require to complete the project.

Wire which is used for securing and for the stems of flowers should be covered, either with ribbon (which may slip) or with Parafilm, which is a self-adhesive tape used by florists.

Milliners wire is used in some projects to define outlines, allowing you to bend the piece into a shape which it then holds. Generally, this wire is covered by stitching over it with an appliqué/satin stitch.

*A selection of essential materials*

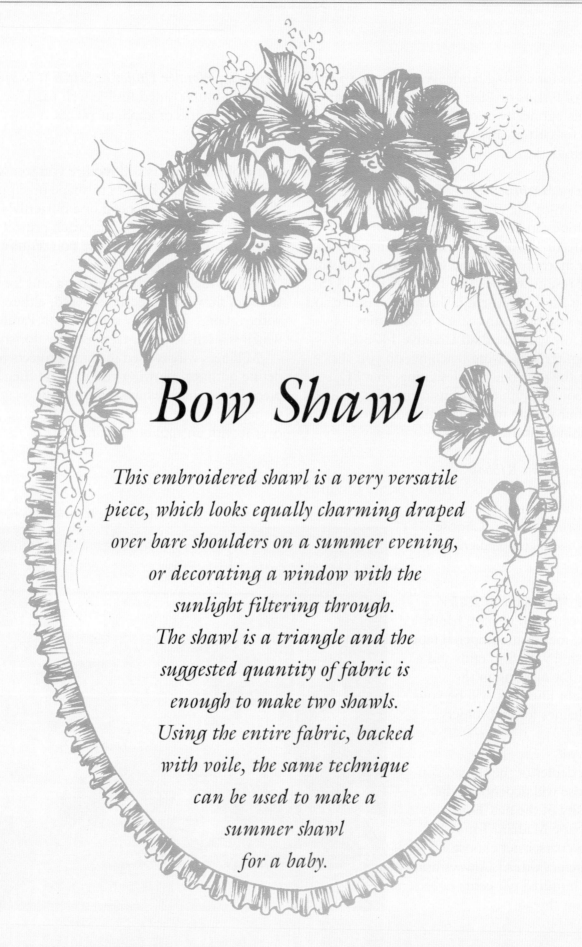

# Bow Shawl

*This embroidered shawl is a very versatile piece, which looks equally charming draped over bare shoulders on a summer evening, or decorating a window with the sunlight filtering through.*
*The shawl is a triangle and the suggested quantity of fabric is enough to make two shawls.*
*Using the entire fabric, backed with voile, the same technique can be used to make a summer shawl for a baby.*

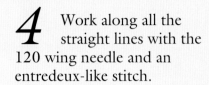

## MATERIALS

*1.5 m (1²/₃ yd) of cotton net tulle*

*Fabric Stiffener*

*Fray Stoppa*

*blue wipe-off fabric marker pen*

*two reels of Madeira Tanne white cotton thread*

*2.5/80 twin needle*

*120 wing needle*

*six large guipure lace motifs*

*five small lace butterfly motifs*

*10 cm (4 in) of Vliesofix*

*small sharp scissors*

## METHOD

See the bow design on the Pull Out Pattern Sheet.

*1* Cut out a right-angled triangular piece from the tulle with the long side 150 cm (1²/₃ yd) long and the two shorter sides each 100 cm (40 in) long.

*2* Treat the centre area of the triangle where the machine-embroidered bow will fall with fabric stabiliser. Allow the tulle to dry, then iron it flat.

*3* Using the marker pen, trace the bow from the Pattern Sheet on to the stabilised area in the centre of the shawl. Trace in all the straight lines as well, as these form the edges of the wing needle entredeux lacework.

*4* Work along all the straight lines with the 120 wing needle and an entredeux-like stitch.

*5* Work the wavy lines with a cross-like satin stitch.

*6* Work the zigzag lines with an open, double-stitched flower-like design.

*7* Using an appliqué/satin stitch (width 2.0, length 0.25 to 0.3), stitch around the design lines of the bow, knot and tails.

*8* Using a fine open scallop (reduced width 5.5, length 0.25 to 0.3 and pattern length 7.0), follow the appliqué lines of the bow, pivoting so that the edge of each scallop meets the appliqué stitch.

*9* Treat a 10 cm (4 in) area around the entire edge of the shawl with fabric stabiliser. Allow the tulle to dry, then iron it flat.

NOTE: The Pfaff Creative 1475 CD has an eight-directional feed which allows you to place stitches in the machine's permanent memory so that they will form a scalloped edge that is stitched with a scallop. If your machine cannot do this, draw a shaped edge, then guide your machine along the lines that you have drawn.

*The embroidered bow*

*10* Using the twin needle and two reels of white cotton thread, stitch around the entire edge of the shawl with a shaped scallop that forms a scalloped edge (see pages 7-9). Use the twin needle button and the needle-down button to reduce the width of the scallop, making it easier for you to pivot at the corners.

*11* To form a lace edge, following the shape of the scalloped edge, stitch the following:
Row 1: Work a heart satin stitch design 1 cm from the scalloped edge.
Row 2: Work an open scroll-like stitch 1 cm from the heart design (Row 1).
Row 3: Same as Row 1
Row 4: Work a stitch that looks like a fine braid 1 cm from the heart design and using the twin needle.

*12* Wash out the fabric stabiliser. Allow the tulle to dry, then iron it flat, using spray starch.

*13* Iron a piece of Vliesofix to the back of the guipure lace motifs. Experiment with the arrangement of the motifs around the large bow until you are satisfied and then iron them in place. You can stitch them in place with small straight stitches, but this is not necessary as they will not fall off in the wash.

*The lace edge of the shawl*

*14* Treat the outside edge of the scallops around the shawl with the fray stopper. Allow the fabric to dry, then cut away the excess fabric from the outer edges.

*15* Treat the marked areas that are to be cut away in the centre of the bow loops with the fray stopper. Allow the tulle to dry, then cut away the excess fabric.

*16* Wash out the fabric stabiliser. Allow the shawl to dry, then iron it flat.

*The guipure lace motifs are available from Capitol Imports*

# Lace Cushion

*With its delicate embroidery and lace
butterfly motif, this little cushion brings
to mind a gentle and romantic time, far
from today's rush and bustle.
Use your cushion as the ring pillow for a
wedding, a baby pillow, or to
grace that special chair.*

## MATERIALS

*40 cm (16 in) of cotton net tulle*

*50 cm (20 in) of fine cream silk*

*Fabric Stiffener*

*Fray Stoppa*

*blue wipe-off fabric marker pen*

*1 m of 2 cm (1¼ yd of ¾ in) wide insertion lace*

*spray starch*

*50 cm of 2 cm (20 in of ¾ in) wide edging lace*

*one bag of polyester fibre stuffing*

*a lace motif for the centre (an antique one if you can find one)*

*one reel of Madeira Tanne cotton thread*

**For the antique dye**
*two tea bags*

*two tablespoons of instant coffee*

*two tablespoons of white vinegar*

*two litres (three and a half pints) of boiling water*

## METHOD

See the lace-shaping and embroidery design on the Pull Out Pattern Sheet.

**1** From the tulle, cut out a rectangle, 30 cm x 42 cm (12 in x 16¾ in), for the top and a strip for the frill, 7 cm x 3 m (3 in x 3¼ yd). (You will need to piece the strip to achieve this length.) Treat the tulle rectangle with the fabric stabiliser, following the manufacturer's instructions. Allow it to dry, then iron it flat.

**2** From the silk, cut out two 30 cm (12 in) squares for the cushion back. The centre back edges will be turned under for 5 cm (2 in) and overlap for 5 cm (2 in) to form an overlapping opening at the back of the cushion.

**3** From the silk, cut two rectangles, 28 cm x 42 cm (11 in x 16¾ in), for the insertion cover. Place the two pieces together with right sides facing and stitch around three sides, leaving one short side open. Turn the cover to the right side. Stuff, taking care not to overstuff. Stitch the opening closed.

**4** Join the frill sections into one long strip. Treat the strip with the fabric stabiliser. Allow the tulle to dry, then iron it flat. Using a fine open scallop, stitch along one edge of the frill. Treat the edge of the scallops

with the fray stopper, allow the tulle to dry, then cut away the excess tulle from the edge.

**5** Use a computer-designed stitch for the lacework as it has the appearance of hand-embroidered net threadwork. If this is not possible, use the largest and most open embroidery stitch built-in to your sewing machine. Stitch this along the length of the frill. Wash out the fabric stabiliser.

**6** Mix the ingredients for the antique dye. Dip the frill strip in the dye, rinse it in cold water and set it aside to dry.

**7** Iron the tulle piece for the cushion top. Trace the lace-shaping design from the Pattern Sheet on to this piece, using the marker pen.

**8** Iron the lace, using the spray starch. To shape the lace over the curved lines, gather the inside edge slightly and pull gently on the outside edge at the curves. Begin shaping the lace over the four small half-circles first. Cut the edging lace into four equal lengths. Shape these over the half-circles with the picket edge to the outside. Pin and stitch the lace in place, just inside both edges, with a small straight stitch.

**9** Shape the insertion lace over all the curved lines in the centre of the cushion, making sure you cover all the raw edges of the lace. Pin the lace in place as before and then stitch it down just inside both edges as for the half-circles of edging lace.

**10** Working on the wrong side, cut the tulle down the centre, behind the inserted lace. Clip into the curves, then press the cut fabric edges flat back over the lace edge. Using a small zigzag stitch and working on the wrong side of the tulle, stitch these cut fabric edges down, just inside the outside edge of the lace. From the back, cut away any excess fabric on the outside edge of the lace. (This step is not absolutely necessary as the tulle is very fine and cannot be seen through the lace from the right side of the work.)

**11** Centre the lace motif on the cushion top and pin it in place. Stitch it down with a small zigzag stitch. Cut away the excess fabric from behind the motif.

**12** In the centre of the four half-circles, work a satin stitch heart on either side of a scroll-like stitch. In the four inside corners of the lace shaping, work a large open stitch pattern, mirror-reversing your pattern when necessary.

**13** Wash out the fabric stabiliser, then dye the top to match the frill strip.

**14** Iron all the pieces flat. Gather up the frill strip to fit around the outside edge of the top, using a straight stitch lengthened to 5 or 6 and tighten your top tension to 7 or 8.

**15** Divide the frill into four equal lengths, marking each quarter point with a pin. With right sides together and raw edges even, pin the frill to the cushion top, placing a pin at each corner. Stitch the frill into place.

**16** To make the back, turn in 1 cm (½ in) on the raw edges of both centre back edges of the cushion back pieces. Turn and stitch 4 cm (1½ in) hems on both edges. Overlap the edges and pin the overlap in place.

**17** With right sides together and raw edges even, join the cushion front and back, stitching around all four sides. Turn the cover to the right side. Place the cushion insert inside the cover through the back opening.

*The lace-shaping design and frilled edge*

# Christening Gown

Delicate and dreamy, this christening
gown and bonnet are destined to
become family heirlooms.
In fact, it is hard to believe that
they are not already antiques. The secret
lies in the soft sepia colour of the net,
achieved by using a dye which you
mix yourself from all natural,
traditional ingredients.

## MATERIALS

2 m (2¼yd) of cotton net tulle

Fabric Stiffener

Fray Stoppa

10 cm (4 in) of Vliesofix

10 cm (4 in) of fine silk shantung

blue wipe-off fabric marker pen

tracing paper

pencil

two reels of Madeira Tanne white cotton thread

4.5 m of 3 mm (5 yd of ¼ in) wide satin ribbon in a suitable colour

1 m of 5 mm (1¼ yd of ¼ in)wide satin ribbon in the same colour

2.5/80 twin needle

70/80 sewing machine needles

three small buttons

small sharp scissors

**For the antique dye**
two tea bags

two tablespoons of instant coffee

two tablespoons of white vinegar

two litres (three and a half pints) of boiling water

## METHOD

### Christening Gown

See the christening gown pattern, the heart and the bow pattern on the Pull Out Pattern Sheet. 1 cm (½ in) seams allowed around all the pattern pieces.

*1* Trace the pattern pieces from the Pattern Sheet on to the tulle, using the marker pen. Cut out the sleeves; front and back bodices; and two rectangles for the front and back skirts, each 70 cm x 80 cm (28 in x 32 in).

*2* Following the manufacturer's instructions, treat the bottom 30 cm (12 in) of both the skirt pieces with the fabric stabiliser. Allow the tulle to dry, then iron it flat.

*3* The front and back skirts are made in the same way. The embroidery on the bottom of the skirt is done with the twin needle and two reels of thread,

using a shaped scallop design.

The hemline has been created with the Pfaff Creative 1475 CD which has an eight-way directional feed, allowing you to step out the scallop stitch automatically.

If this is not possible on your machine, divide the front and back skirt pieces each into five equal panels. Lightly mark the centre line down each panel then draw a straight line along the hemline, 6 cm (2½ in) up from the bottom edge. Use the marker pen for all these markings.

Shape the peaked edge by drawing a 10 cm (4 in) line from the centre point at the bottom of each panel up to the 6 cm (2½ in) mark on both side edges of each panel. (Figure 1) Mark a point on each panel, 5 cm (2 in) up from the bottom peak. Trace both outlines of the heart pattern from the Pattern Sheet, centring it in each panel and with the point of the heart on the 5 cm (2 in) mark.

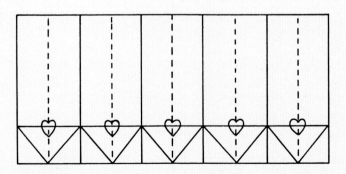

*Figure 1*

**4** Treat the outside edges of the scallops with the fray stopper. Allow the tulle to dry, then carefully cut away the excess tulle from the outer edge.

**5** Using the twin needle and a feather stitch (width 4, length 4), stitch around the marked outside and inside outlines of all ten hearts.

**6** Using a satin stitch flower and leaf design, work around the heart, inside the two rows of feather stitch. Work the two sides of the heart separately, starting at the top and working first down the right side to the bottom. Then start at the top of the heart again and, mirror-reversing, work down the left side in the same way.

**7** Trace the bow from the Pattern Sheet ten times on to the paper side of the Vliesofix. Iron the ten Vliesofix bows on to the wrong side of the silk shantung. Cut out the bows, remove the paper backing and iron them on to the right side of the embroidered tulle, in the centre of the inner heart outline.

**8** Using a fine satin stitch (width 1.5, length 0.25), appliqué the bows in place, including the outline at the top of the bow loops.

**9** With right sides facing, join one skirt side seam.

*The heart and bow design*

**10** Mark a line around the skirt, 1.5 cm (³⁄₄ in) from the top of the hearts. Stitch an open flower and leaf pattern along this marked line.

**11** For the 6 cm (2¹⁄₂ in) wide embroidered border, stitch the following rows:
Row 1: Work a fine scallop stitch with an embroidered heart centred in each scallop.
Rows 2 and 3: Centred in the border, stitch a half-circle design down one side, then mirror-reverse the pattern, matching up the sides to form circles, and work down the other side of the centre panel.
Row 4: As Row 1.

**12** Wash out the fabric stabiliser. Allow the tulle to dry, then iron it flat.

**13** Treat a 20 cm (8 in) wide panel down the centre front of the skirt with the fabric stabiliser, starting from the

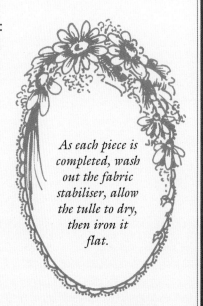

*As each piece is completed, wash out the fabric stabiliser, allow the tulle to dry, then iron it flat.*

top edge of the embroidered border you have just worked to the top edge of the skirt.

**14** Draw a line down the centre of the skirt front. Embroider one side of the centre front panel as follows, noting that in this case the rows are vertical rows (Figure 2): Rows 1 and 2: Using the twin needle, work large scrolls in satin stitch, placing the rows 4 cm (1½ in) apart and mirror-reversing their direction. Rows 3 and 4: Using the single needle and beginning 1 cm (½ in) in from Row 1, stitch a half-circle design down the panel. Mirror-reverse the pattern for Row 4 to form circles. Row 5: Stitch a large open design. Row 6: Stitch the same design as on the bottom of the skirt. For the other side of the centre front panel, repeat Rows 1 to 5, mirror-reversing where necessary.

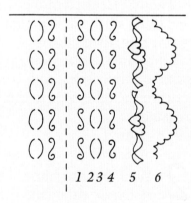

Figure 2

*Twin needle large satin stitch scrolls*

*Single needle half-circle*

*Large open design*

*Same stitch as on the skirt hem*

**15** Using a large open stitch and starting from the left-hand side of the vertical centre front panel, stitch around the skirt 1 cm (½ in) up from the bottom embroidered panel.

**16** Join the remaining skirt side seam.

**17** Cut down 10 cm (4 in) in the skirt centre back for the placket opening.

**18** Wash out the fabric stabiliser. Allow the tulle to dry, then iron it flat.

**19** Treat the front bodice with the fabric stabiliser. Allow the tulle to dry, then mark the centre front line with the marker pen.

**20** Stitch matching half-circle designs down the centre front bodice with twin needle work on either side as for the centre front panel of the skirt.

**21** Stitch the same twin needle work as in Step 14 down either side of the bodice, from the centre of the shoulder seams. Down the centre of these two panels, stitch over the 3 mm (¼ in) wide satin ribbon with an encasing stitch to look like it has been threaded through wide entredeux or faggoting.

**22** Join the front and back shoulders with small French seams.

**23** Using the twin needle, stitch around the neck edge with the same stitch as used on the bottom skirt edge. Treat the edge of the tulle with the fray stopper. Allow the tulle to dry, then cut away the excess tulle from the edge.

**24** Make a narrow hem on each side of the centre back opening, then turn back the facing to fit. Finish off the back skirt placket with a small piece of tulle or ribbon facing, handstitched over the raw edge.

**25** Treat a 10 cm (4 in) strip down the centre of each sleeve and a 5 cm (2 in) strip around the bottom edge of the sleeves with the fabric stabiliser. Allow the tulle to dry, then iron it flat.

**26** Repeat the same panel as stitched down the centre front bodice down each sleeve. Stitch the edges with twin needle work to match the neck edge of the bodice. Treat the edge of the tulle with the fray stopper. Allow the tulle to dry, then cut away the excess tulle from the edge.

**27** Along a line 5 cm (2 in) from the bottom of the sleeves, stitch an encasing stitch over the 3 mm

*The bodice*

(¼ in) wide ribbon, the same as stitched on the front bodice. Pull up the ribbon to gather up the sleeve ends.

**28** Cut out the underarm shapes.

**29** Gather up the skirt to fit the bodice. Attach the skirt to the bodice at the waist, matching the back plackets and centre front panels.

**30** Gather up the sleeve heads to fit the armholes. Join the underarm sleeve seams, then sew the sleeves into the armholes.

**31** With the remaining 3 mm (¼ in) wide ribbon, tie two small bows with love knots in the tails. Stitch one on either side of the bodice at the end of the ribbon insertion.

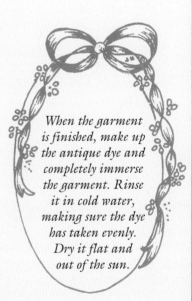

*When the garment is finished, make up the antique dye and completely immerse the garment. Rinse it in cold water, making sure the dye has taken evenly. Dry it flat and out of the sun.*

## Bonnet

*1* Using leftover fabric, cut the following pieces: one strip 7 cm x 50 cm (3 in x 20 in) for the frill; one strip 6 cm x 28 cm (2½ in x 11 in) for the embroidered panel; one strip 6 cm x 50 cm (2½ in x 20 in) for the piece to be puffed; one strip 10 cm x 28 cm (4 in x 11 in) for the back panel.

*2* Treat all the pieces, except for the piece to be puffed, with the fabric stabiliser.

*3* Using the same stitch as on the edge of the sleeves and the twin needle, stitch down the edge of the frill strip. Treat the edge with the fray stopper. Allow the tulle to dry, then cut away the excess tulle on the edge. Wash out the fabric stabiliser. Dye the strip, allow it to dry and gather up the frill.

*4* For the embroidered panel, stitch as for the centre panel of the sleeves. Wash out the fabric stabiliser and dye the piece.

*5* Dye the piece for puffing. Allow the tulle to dry, then iron it flat. Using a straight stitch (length 6, upper tension 8) gather up both sides to make perfect puffing every time.

*6* For the back panel, work the following rows:
Row 1: Using the twin needle, work scallops along the bottom edge. Treat with the fray stopper. Allow the tulle to dry, then cut away the excess tulle on the edge.
Row 2: Come in 2 cm (¾ in) from Row 1 and, using the same encasing stitch as on the christening gown bodice, cover a length of 3 mm (¼ in) wide ribbon.
Row 3: Come in 2 cm (¾ in) from Row 2 and, using the twin needle, stitch the same design as on the frill edge.
Row 4: Come in 1 cm (½ in) from Row 3 and stitch an open flower and leaf design.

*7* Wash out the fabric stabiliser. Dye the piece, allow the tulle to dry, then iron it flat.

*8* Join all the pieces together in the following order: frill, embroidered panel, puffed piece, back panel. Pull up the back panel and tie the ribbon with a small bow.

*9* Pleat the sides of the frill and attach a length of the 5 mm (¼ in) wide satin ribbon to either side of the bonnet, over the pleating.

For the bonnet, wash out the fabric stabiliser first, then dye the long piece before puffing it. Embroider and dye the other three pieces before the fabric stabiliser is washed out.

*The bonnet*

# Lace Fan

There was a time when no well-bred young lady would venture out without a fan, behind which she would hide her blushes and flutter her lashes. Bring back those romantic days with this lovely fan of embroidered tulle, displayed on a stand or framed behind glass. Tulle is one hundred per cent cotton, so it can be dyed.

## MATERIALS

*fan shape*

*30 cm x 45 cm (12 in x 18 in) of cotton net tulle (or the required amount if your fan shape is larger or smaller than 40 cm [16 in] across)*

*blue wipe-off fabric marker pen*

*one reel of Madeira Tanne cotton thread*

*Fray Stoppa*

*Fabric Stiffener*

*small sharp scissors*

*tassel*

## METHOD

*1* Treat the tulle with fabric stabiliser, following the manufacturer's instructions. Peel the nylon lace off your fan shape in one piece. Using the discarded nylon lace as your pattern, trace the outline on to the piece of tulle with the marker pen. Remember to allow an extra 2 cm (³⁄₄ in) all around for the shrinkage caused by the embroidery.

*2* Mark the centre of the fan shape and draw a vertical line from the top to the bottom of the fan through this point. Draw in lines dividing each half of the fan into three equal segments (six segments in all). Make sure the lines are straight and accurately drawn as these are your guidelines for the embroidery. (Figure 1)

*Figure 1*

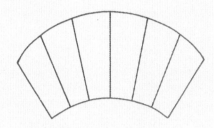

*3* Each segment dividing line is embroidered in the same way:

❋ The centre row is stitched with a filled-in satin stitch heart and circle design.
❋ On each side of the hearts, work a hem stitch design using the 120 wing needle.
❋ On each side of the hem stitch, work a filled-in satin stitch scallop design.

This design can be worked along the entire length of the segment dividing lines, or can stop halfway up with a large embroidery stitch just above the halfway mark to add interest.

*4* Work around the top edge of the fan with a maxi-scallop, with a reduced open scallop around the outside edge of the maxi-scallops. Work in a straight line across the inside bottom edge of the maxi-scallops with the same heart stitch as is used on the centre of each segment dividing line. (Figure 2)

*The fan embroidery*

*The scalloped edge of the fan*

**5** The bottom and side edges of the fan shape are worked with the same filled-in satin stitch scallop as is used on either side of the segment dividing line.

**6** Treat all the edges with the fray stopper. Allow the tulle to dry, then carefully cut out the fan shape around all the scalloped edges. Wash out the fabric stabiliser. Allow the tulle to dry, then iron it flat.

*Figure 2*

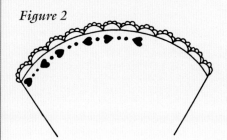

**7** Arrange the fan struts so that every second strut aligns with an embroidered line on the tulle, then glue the struts in place. When you assemble the fan, make sure one end strut is under and the other one is on top of the net. Do not use too much glue as any excess will show through the tulle.

**8** Attach the tassel. Allow the glue to dry completely before using the fan.

NOTE: The heart and bow motif on this fan was achieved with the aid of the PC Designer Software that allows you to design on a PC and then stitch it using your Pfaff Creative 1475 CD sewing machine. If this is not possible, trace the design on to the fabric and then work it freehand in a hoop.

*Most craft shops sell inexpensive fans. To make this unique fan, simply strip the covering off a purchased fan.*

# Lace Butterfly

This little butterfly will make a lovely adornment as a brooch for a special dress, a delicate mobile or a decoration with a touch of whimsy. To give an added dimension, make a smaller butterfly in exactly the same way and place it on top of the larger one.

## MATERIALS

*20 cm (8 in) square of cotton net tulle*

*15 cm (6 in) embroidery hoop with the inside ring bound*

*one reel of Madeira Tanne cotton thread*

*50 cm (20 in) of covered milliners wire*

*blue wipe-off fabric marker pen*

*Fray Stoppa*

*Fabric Stiffener*

*sharp scissors*

*wire cutters (never use scissors to cut wire)*

## METHOD

See the butterfly pattern and embroidery design on the Pull Out Pattern Sheet.

*1* Treat the tulle with fabric stabiliser, following the manufacturer's instructions. Trace the butterfly design from the Pattern Sheet on to the centre of the square of tulle, using the marker pen.

*2* Place the tulle in the embroidery hoop and set your sewing machine for freehand embroidery with the feed dogs down and the presser foot off. If you are not using a Pfaff sewing machine, you will need to unscrew the shank of your foot. Engage the tension and bring the bobbin thread to the top of your work. Secure the beginning of the stitching by working three small stitches on the spot.

*3* Stitch three rows of straight stitch around all the lines on the butterfly design. Try to keep these rows as close together as possible without overlapping.

*4* While the tulle is still in the hoop and your machine is set to freehand embroidery, embroider tiny circles (turning both right and left) to fill in the body of the butterfly and the oval shapes in the wings.

*5* Take your work out of the hoop and iron it if necessary. Raise the feed dogs on your sewing machine and return the machine to normal sewing mode with the open-toed presser foot.

*6* Stitch the straight lines which are the veins in the butterfly's wings with a small satin stitch embroidery design. Choose a stitch that suits from your sewing machine's repertoire of built-in stitches.

*7* Stitch around the entire outside edge of the wings and the edge of the filled-in ovals in the wings, using an open or closed scallop with a reduced width, length and pattern length (width 4.5, length 0.25, pattern length 6.0).

*8* Place the milliners wire on the inside edge of the scallops of the wings. Using

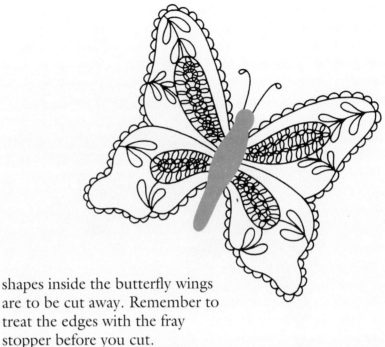

satin stitch (width 2.0, length 0.25), stitch over the wire.

**9** Form a tight U-shape with a 4 cm (1½ in) piece of the milliners wire and work the antennae. Do not worry about shaping the little hook at the end of each antenna at this stage – they can be shaped later. Stitch the milliners wire around the body shape last, making sure that you attach the antennae securely to the body of the butterfly as you go.

**10** Treat the outside edge of the butterfly, including the antennae, with the fray stopper. Allow it to dry.

**11** Cut out the butterfly, making sure you cut carefully around all the scallops. Choose which of the plain net shapes inside the butterfly wings are to be cut away. Remember to treat the edges with the fray stopper before you cut.

**12** When all the cutting is complete, carefully wash out the fabric stabiliser. Allow the butterfly to dry, then shape the wired wings to a pleasing shape. Form a hook on the end of each antenna.

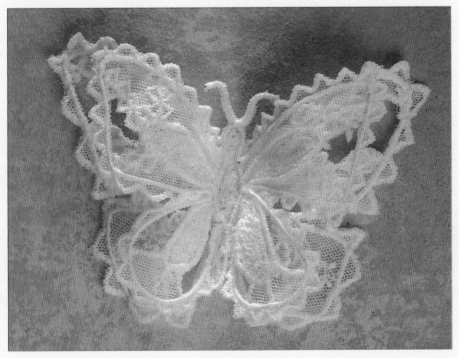

*The butterfly*

# Cradle Set

*Pink, silk-like thread adorns
this charming cradle set with its
heavy lace embroidery effect.
Of course, you can embroider in
blue or any other colour you wish.
This technique can be used in
many different ways for
cushions and fabric trims.*

## MATERIALS

*Fabric Stiffener*

*Fray Stoppa*

*small sharp scissors*

*blue wipe-off fabric marker pen*

*one reel of Madeira Tanne cotton thread*

**For the drape**

*3 m (3¼ yd) of cotton net tulle*

*2 m of 33 mm (2¼ yd of 1¼ in) wide satin ribbon*

**For the skirt**

*9 m (10 yd) of cotton voile (allowing for gathering fabric three times the circumference of this cradle)*

*4 m of 33 mm (4½ yd of 1¼ in) wide satin ribbon*

**For the cradle cover and pillow sham**

*50 cm (20 in) of cotton net tulle for the top*

*50 cm (20 in) of cotton voile or organza for the lining*

*50 cm (20 in) of polyester wadding*

*1 m (1¼ yd) of cotton for backing*

*one reel of Madeira Sticku pink embroidery thread*

## METHOD

### Cradle Drape

**1** Measure the height of the pole that will support the drape, then work out how far down the sides of the cradle you wish the drape to fall from the pole. Remember, you will need to allow twice this measurement. The width of the tulle will be gathered along the pole. Cut a piece of tulle to the length you have calculated.

**2** Treat an 8 cm (3¼ in) wide strip around all the edges of the tulle with fabric stabiliser. Allow the tulle to dry, then iron it flat.

**3** A stepped, open scallop was used to embroider the edge of the net. If you do not have the magic of the Pfaff multi-directional feeding system to assist you, choose a similar scallop and stitch it around the edge. If you particularly want to reproduce the same design that you see here, make a template of the edge shape and trace around it in a repeating design. Stitch along these traced lines. When you have finished the stitching, treat the outside edge with the fray stopper, then cut away the excess tulle on the edge of the scallop design.

**4** Cut the net in half length-ways. Place both pieces together with the wrong sides facing and the raw edges even. Treat an 8 cm (3¼ in) strip along the raw edges with the fabric stabiliser. Using the same stitch as you used around the edge, stitch the raw edges of the two pieces of net together. Treat the outside edge of the scallops with the fray stopper. Allow the tulle to dry, then cut away the excess tulle from the outer edge of the scallops with the scissors.

**5** With a small straight stitch, stitch a casing for the rod to go through, placing the first row of stitching 5 cm (2 in) from the top edge. Thread the drape on to the rod, softly gathering up the fabric.

**6** Tie a large bow on the end of the rod to hold the drape in place, leaving long tails that will fall gracefully down the sides of the drape.

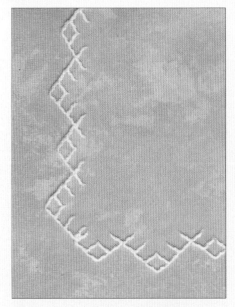

*The lace edge of the cradle drape*

## Cradle Skirt

See the bow and the butterfly designs on the Pull Out Pattern Sheet.

**1** Measure the circumference of the cradle and multiply this length by three in order to calculate the length of fabric you will require. Cut a 10 cm (4 in) wide strip along the length of the fabric and set it aside for the frills on the cover and pillow sham.

**2** Treat a 10 cm (4 in) wide strip along the bottom edge of the skirt fabric with the fabric stabiliser. Allow the fabric to dry, then iron it flat.

**3** Stitch around the edge with a maxi-scallop, stepped out so that two rows of stitching are worked in one. If this is not possible, then the same effect can be achieved by stitching two rows of large scallops as shown in Figure 1.

**4** Treat the inside and outside edge of the top row of scallops with the fray stopper. Allow the fabric to dry, then cut away the excess fabric on the outside edge of the scallops. Cut away the fabric inside the top row of scallops as well, so that it resembles cutwork.

**5** Treat a 50 cm (20 in) square on the front of the skirt with the fabric stabiliser. Trace the bow and butterflies for the skirt front from the Pattern

*The complete cradle*

Sheet on to the right side of the fabric, using the marker pen. Cut a piece of tulle to the approximate size of the design from the tulle allowed for the pillow and cradle cover. Pin this piece of tulle to the wrong side of the voile, beneath the bow and butterfly designs, placing the pins on the right side of the fabric.

On the right side of the fabric, stitch over the design lines with small straight stitches,

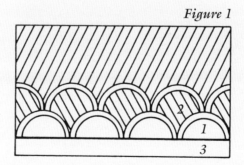

*Figure 1*

☐ Cut away

☐ Cut away

*Row 1: Open satin stitch scallop*
*Row 2: Open satin stitch scallop*
*Row 3: Small satin stitch*

attaching the tulle to the voile and keeping both fabrics flat and smooth.

6 With the small sharp scissors, cut away the voile from inside the loops and ties of the bow, allowing the tulle to show through. Working from the wrong side, cut away the tulle from the inside of the bow and the knot. With a filled-in scallop design, stitch over the design lines, covering the cut edges as you go.

7 Make the butterflies in the same way, cutting away the voile so that one butterfly is in net with the body and ovals in voile, and the other one is reversed with the body and ovals in tulle.

8 Wash out the fabric stabiliser. Allow the fabric to dry and then iron it flat.

9 Join the centre back seam. Measure the desired length of the skirt. Neaten the raw edge at the top and then fold down 6 cm (2½ in) to form a casing for the elastic and allowing for a 4 cm (1½ in) frill at the top.

10 Measure the length for the elastic so that it fits firmly around the cradle. Thread the elastic through the casing and stitch the ends of the elastic together.

11 Adjust the gathering around the cradle so that the bow and butterflies are in the centre front.

12 Securely attach 1 m (1¼ yd) of ribbon to the skirt at each corner of the crib. Tie a bow around the corner posts of the cradle to keep the skirt in place. Leave the tails long so that they trail gracefully down the sides of the skirt.

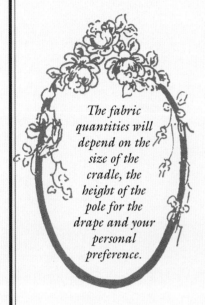

*The fabric quantities will depend on the size of the cradle, the height of the pole for the drape and your personal preference.*

*The embroidered bow*

## Cradle Cover and Pillow Sham

See the bow and swag designs on the Pull Out Pattern Sheet. To calculate the size of the cradle cover, measure the size you wish the pillow sham to be, then subtract this from the total length of your cradle.

*1* Treat the 10 cm (4 in) wide voile frill piece with the fabric stabiliser. Allow the voile to dry, then iron it flat.

*2* Using the pink Sticku embroidery thread, stitch a decorative edge that matches the tulle drape along one long side of the frill. Treat the outside edge of the scallops with the fray stopper. Allow the fabric to dry, then cut away the excess fabric on the outside edge of the scallops.

*3* Cut out tulle pieces to the sizes you have calculated for the cradle cover and pillow sham. Cut out the voile lining, wadding and cotton or polycotton backing to the same sizes. Put the voile lining, wadding and backing pieces aside.

*4* Treat the tulle with the fabric stabiliser. Allow it to dry, then iron it flat. Fold both pieces of tulle down the centre lengthways, then fold them down the centre lengthways again, dividing the tulle into quarters. Draw in these lines with the marker pen; they

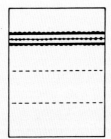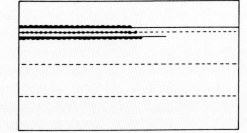

*Figure 2*

will be your centre guidelines for embroidery.

*5* Stitch a filled-in scallop design down both sides of each marked line and 2 cm (³⁄₄ in) apart. Finish with a satin stitch along the base of the scallops.

*6* Stitch a filled-in machine-embroidery stitch down the centre of each of the panels formed in Step 5. (Figure 2)

*7* Pin the voile piece under the tulle piece. Fold the tulle and voile together into quarters to determine the centre point of each side. Using the marker pen, trace the bow and swag designs from the Pattern Sheet on to opposite sides of the pillow sham. Trace a bow and swag design on to each end and on opposite sides of the cradle cover. In each case, centre the design 5 cm (2 in) from the edges. (Figure 3)

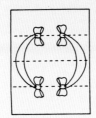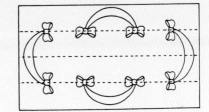

*Figure 3*

**8** Straight stitch around all the design lines on the bow and swag. Cut the tulle away from the top. Appliqué/ satin stitch around all the lines, covering the cut edges. Using a small satin stitch scallop design, reduced in width, length and pattern length, stitch around the design. Make sure the bottom of the scallops meets the appliqué/ satin stitch and pivot the stitching at the corners.

**9** For both the cradle cover and the pillow sham, pin all the fabric layers together in the following order: cotton or polycotton backing fabric, wadding, voile and tulle. From this point onwards, both pieces are made in the same way, so only one instruction will be given and it will apply to both.

**10** Working out from the centre, baste all the layers together with a straight stitch (length 6.0) and loosen off the upper tension so that this stitching can be removed easily. Work this stitching in all directions of the compass. Stitch around the outside edge in the same way to secure all the layers.

**11** Using the white thread, quilt around the inside of the embroidered bow and swag design, just inside the pink satin stitch.

**12** Gather up the frill strip to fit around the outside edge. (Remember you need to have a frill for the cradle cover and another one for the pillow sham.) Divide the length of the frill into quarters and mark the points with a pin. With the right side of work facing up, the right side of the frill and the work together, raw edges even and the pins matching the corners, attach the frill.

**13** Cut out the backing for the cradle cover and pillow sham. With right sides facing, attach the backings, stitching around the outside edges and leaving an opening on one short end for turning.

**14** Turn the work right side out and slipstitch the opening closed.

**15** Wash out the fabric stabiliser. Allow the pillow sham and cover to dry, then iron them flat.

**16** Make some pretty machine-embroidered sheets to complete the set.

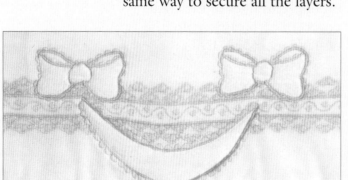

*The cradle cover embroidery*

*The cradle cover
and pillow sham*

# Fan Skirt
# and
# Camisole

*Team this delicate camisole with a pair
of French knickers for an exquisite
lingerie set. Use a commercial pattern
for the knickers and repeat a part of the
tulle appliqué on the front legs.
The embroidered skirt piece also
makes a simple but very elegant
European window
treatment.*

## MATERIALS

*3.5 m (4 yd) of Swiss cotton voile*

*50 cm (20 in) of cotton net tulle*

*Fabric Stiffener*

*Fray Stoppa*

*small sharp scissors*

*blue wipe-off fabric marker pen*

*four reels of Madeira Tanne white cotton thread*

*20 m of 3 mm (22 yd of ¼ in) wide white satin ribbon*

*2.5/80 twin needle*

*small piece of heavy interfacing for the waistband (optional)*

*20 cm (8 in) Vliesofix*

*20 cm (8 in) of white taffeta*

*one 1.5 cm (¾ in) button*

## METHOD

See the camisole pattern and the embroidery designs on the Pull Out Pattern Sheet. 1.5 cm (¾ in) seams are allowed on the flat seams and 5 mm (¼ in) seam allowances on the French seams.

The camisole pattern is given in sizes 8, 10 and 12. The fan skirt is a multi-size pattern; adjust it as you need to.

### Skirt

*1* Cut a strip 25 cm x 3.5 m (10 in x 4 yd) for the skirt frill from the length of the voile. Cut this piece in half lengthways, then seam the two pieces together to form a strip approximately 12.5 cm x 7 m (5 in x 8 yd). Treat a 6 cm (2½ in) border on one long edge of the joined strip with the fabric stabiliser. Set the strip aside to dry.

*2* Cut off 2.6 m (2⅞ in) of the voile for the skirt. Divide and, with the marker pen, mark the length of the piece into six equal panels. Trace the oval outline from the Pattern Sheet

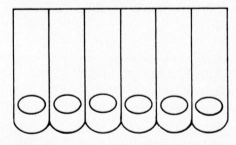

*Figure 1*

on to the centre of each panel, 10 cm (4 in) from the bottom edge.

*3* Draw a large scallop on the hem of the skirt so that the peak of each scallop lies exactly in the centre of two ovals. (Figure 1)

*4* Treat a 30 cm (12 in) border at the bottom of the skirt with the fabric stabiliser. Allow the voile to dry, then iron it flat.

*5* Using the twin needle and two reels of white thread, stitch an open scallop along the scalloped hemline of the skirt.

*6* Working 1 cm (½ in) up from the row of scallops, stitch over the 3 mm (¼ in) wide white ribbon with an encasing stitch. The effect should be the same as if the ribbon was threaded through faggoting. At the peaks of the scallops, simply fold the ribbon over to maintain the shape.

*7* Still using the twin needle, work a single straight stitch design that forms little circles along the edge of the enclosed ribbon. (Figure 2)

*8* Treat the scalloped edge with the fray stopper. Allow the voile to dry, then cut away the excess fabric on the outside edge of the scallops.

*Figure 2*

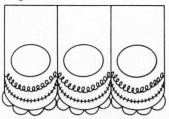

〜〜    *Open scallop*
++++++    *Encasing stitch*
ℓℓℓℓℓℓ    *Twin needle work*

**9** Embroider the frill strip in the same way as the skirt hem. When the stitching is completed, treat the outside edge of the scallop with the fray stopper. Allow the voile to dry, then cut away the excess fabric on the outside edge as before.

**10** Cut out seven tulle ovals, following the oval pattern on the Pattern Sheet. Treat them with the fabric stabiliser. Allow the tulle to dry, then carefully iron the ovals, making sure you don't distort their shape.

**11** Trace the fan pattern from the Pattern Sheet on to the centre of each tulle oval, using the marker pen. Each fan is worked in the same way. Work the top 2 cm ($^3/_4$ in) of the fan with a filled-in stitch which looks like tiny circles. The effect is like freehand embroidery, but it is much easier to do this way.

**12** Down each strut and at the side edges of the fan, stitch over a length of 3 mm ($^1/_4$ in) wide ribbon with an encasing stitch as for the frill and skirt. In between each strut, stitch an open flower design. Work a filled-in scallop along the bottom edge of the 2 cm ($^3/_4$ in) filled-in section at the top of the fan. Stitch around the top of the fan with an appliqué/satin stitch, then stitch an open scallop along the top.

**13** Trace the bow pattern for the bottom of the fan six times on to the paper backing of the Vliesofix. Iron the Vliesofix on to the wrong side of the taffeta and carefully cut out the bows. Peel the paper backing off the bows just before you are ready to use them. Iron the bows in place at the base of the fan. Appliqué the bows in place with a satin stitch.

*This tulle appliqué work would make a beautiful tablecloth for a special table in a bay window.*

**The skirt hem and frill**

*The skirt waist*

**14** Place one net oval over each oval drawn on the skirt panels on the right side of the work. Straight stitch the net ovals in place, then satin stitch around the ovals on the inside edge. On the outside edge, stitch a filled-in scallop, pivoting around the oval to keep the outline fluid. Working from the back of the work, carefully cut away the voile from the back of the net ovals.

**15** Join the centre back seam of the skirt with a flat seam, leaving a 10 cm (4 in) opening at the waist edge. Neaten the raw edges by overlocking or zigzagging. Press the seam allowances open, including the seam allowances of the open section.

**16** Join the short ends of the frill strip with a flat seam. Neaten the raw edges of the seam allowances as before and press the seam allowances open. Gather the frill strip to fit the scalloped hemline of the skirt. With right sides together and raw edges even, stitch the frill in place. Trim the seam allowances and neaten the raw edges as before.

**17** Cut a 10 cm (4 in) wide strip of voile to fit your waist plus an allowance for overlaps and closures. Interface the strip if you like a firmer waistband. Stitch three rows of an encasing stitch over 3 mm (1/4 in) wide ribbon along the centre of the waistband. Leaving a 1 m (1 1/4 yd) tail of ribbon free, begin at the centre front and work around the right-hand side to the centre back. Leaving a 1 m (1 1/4 yd) tail of ribbon free at the centre front, work another row of the encasing stitch, beginning at the centre front and mirror-reversing the stitching around the left-hand side to the centre back. Make three complete rows of this stitching so you have six 1 m (1 1/4 yd) lengths of ribbon at the centre front to tie into a bunch. (Figure 3)

*Figure 3*

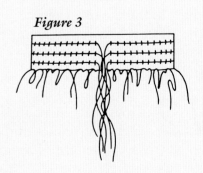

18 Gather the skirt to fit the waistband. With right sides together, stitch the gathered edge of the skirt to one long side of the waistband. Neaten the other long side of the waistband by your preferred method. Fold the waistband over double with right sides together and stitch the short ends and overlaps. Turn the waistband to the right side and slipstitch the neatened edge over the gathering.

19 Make a buttonhole and sew on a button to close the waistband or use hooks and eyes if you prefer.

20 Wash out the fabric stabiliser and allow the skirt to dry before ironing it.

*The oval and fan embroidery on the skirt*

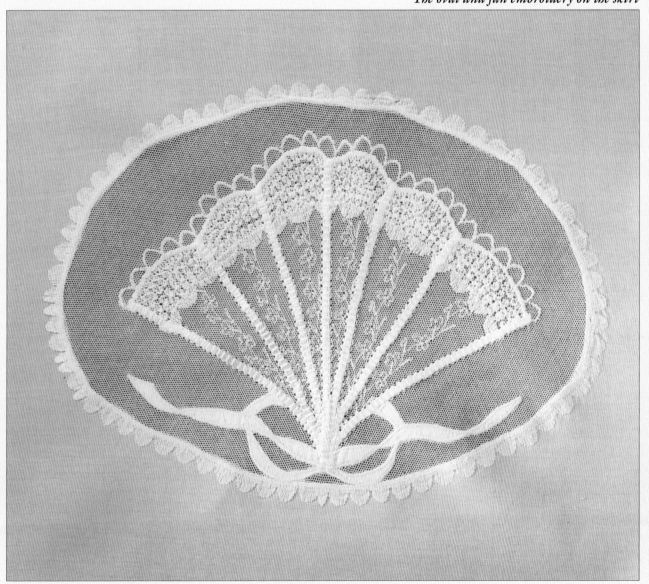

## Camisole

*1* Cut out the front and back camisole following the pattern on the Pattern Sheet. Note that you will need two fronts and two backs because the camisole is made from double fabric so that it is not too sheer.

*2* Stitch the darts in the camisole front and the front lining.

*3* With right sides facing, join the side seams of the top and of the lining. Press all the seams open. Place the camisole and lining together with right sides facing and side seams matching. Stitch around the bottom edge. Trim the seam and turn the camisole to the right side. Press. Pin the upper edges of the camisole and lining together and from here on treat them as a single layer. Treat a 2 cm (³/₄ in) border around the top raw edges with fabric stabiliser. Allow it to dry, then iron it flat.

*4* Using an open scallop, stitch around the top edge of the camisole. Treat the outside edge of the scallops with the fray stopper. Allow the fabric to dry, then cut away the excess fabric on the outside edge.

*5* Work another fan pattern in the same way as for the skirt. Treat the outside edge of the fan with the fray stopper. Allow the tulle to dry, then cut it out very carefully.

*6* Position the fan in the centre front of the camisole so that the scalloped edge of the top of the fan comes up slightly above the scalloped top edge of the camisole. (Figure 4)

*7* Appliqué the fan in place on the camisole by satin stitching down the sides and over the first curve on either side on the top of the fan.

*8* Trace the large double bow on to the paper side of the Vliesofix. Iron the bow on to a piece of taffeta, then cut out the bow. Peel the paper off the back of the Vliesofix, centre the bow at the base of the fan and iron it in place. Stitch around all the edges of the bow with a small appliqué/satin stitch.

*9* On the wrong side, cut away both layers of voile from the back of the fan, cutting

*Figure 4*

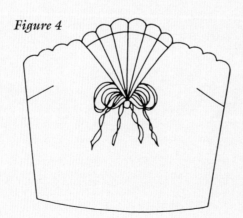

*The fan and bow embroidery on the camisole*

just inside the outer edges of the side struts.

**10** On the wrong side of the work, cut away a single layer of voile from the back of the large loops of the bow.

**11** For the shoulder straps, cut 8 cm (3 ¼ in) wide strips of stabilised voile to the length required. Fold the strips over double and on each side work a scallop to match the one along the top of the cami-sole. Treat the outer edges with the fray stopper. Allow the fabric to dry, then cut away the excess fabric on the outer edges. You can finish the straps by stitching an encasing stitch over a length of 3 mm (¼ in) wide ribbon down the centre of each strap.

If you prefer, you can simply stitch two lengths of ribbon in place for shoulder straps to finish off the camisole.

**12** Wash out the fabric stabiliser. Allow the camisole to dry, then iron it carefully.

# Doll's Dress

Fine hand-embroidered net was the traditional way to dress an exquisite porcelain doll. These days, the time factor makes this a difficult tradition to follow, so here is a way to re-create the spectacular effect using a modern sewing machine.

## MATERIALS

*1 m (1¼ yd) of cotton net tulle for the dress*

*50 cm (20 in) of cotton organza or voile for the petticoat and panties*

*blue wipe-off fabric marker pen*

*Fabric Stiffener*

*Fray Stoppa*

*6 m of 2 cm (6½ yd of ¾ in) wide white cotton insertion lace*

*13 m of 3 mm (14½ yd of ¼ in) wide pink satin ribbon*

*two reels of Madeira Tanne white cotton thread*

*one reel of Madeira Sticku pink embroidery thread*

*six small buttons*

*30 cm (12 in) of narrow elastic*

*spray starch*

*small sharp scissors*

**Cut away**

**Cut away**

## METHOD

See the dress, petticoat and panties patterns on the Pull Out Pattern Sheet. Allow 1 cm (½ in) seam allowances around all pattern pieces.

This pattern and instructions are for a 51 to 56 cm (20 to 22 in) doll.

The bonnet pattern is an adaptation of the Easy Sew Designs pattern, number BHD 561, from Brown House Dolls and is readily available.

## Petticoat

*1* Using the marker pen, trace the pattern from the Pattern Sheet on to the organza or voile. Cut out the skirt and bodice.

*2* Sew the side seams of the skirt.

*3* Cut down a 6 cm (2½ in) opening in the centre back of the skirt. Cut a strip of fabric, 2 cm x 15 cm (¾ in x 6 in), for the placket. Turn under 5 mm (¼ in) down one long side of the placket strip. With right sides together, sew the raw edge of the placket strip to the back opening, pivoting at the lowest point. Turn the placket strip to the wrong side

and slipstitch it in place on the skirt. Fold the placket to one side and sew diagonally across the base of the placket to hold it in place.

*4* Treat a 4 cm (1½ in) border all around the bottom of the skirt with the fabric stabiliser.

The edge of the petticoat has been designed to give a cutwork effect, made possible with the aid of the Pfaff PC Designer Software, which allows two rows to be stitched in one action. If this is not possible for you, choose an open satin stitch scallop and stitch one row right around the circular hem of the petticoat 3 cm (1¼ in) from the edge. Work a second row of stitches on top of this first row to give the 'brick' effect in the pattern.

A small satin stitch has been worked along the straight inside edge of the scallops to give the lace an edge. Treat the edge row (or top row) of the scallops with the fray stopper. Allow the fabric to dry, then cut away the excess fabric on the outside edge of the scallops with the scissors.

The inside fabric of the top row of scallops is also cut out to create a lace cutwork appearance. (Figure 1)

*Figure 1*

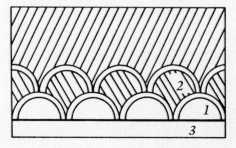

*Row 2: Open satin stitch scallop*

*Row 1: Open satin stitch scallop*

*Row 3: Small satin stitch*

**5** Join the shoulder seams of the bodice and of the lining with right sides facing.

**6** Join the side seams of the bodice and of the lining.

**7** Place the bodice and lining together with right sides facing and raw edges even. Stitch around the neck edge and centre back opening edges. Stitch around the armholes. Trim and clip all the curved seams for ease. Turn the bodice right side out and press.

**8** Gather the top edge of the skirt to fit the bodice. Pin the skirt to the bodice, matching the placket on the skirt back to the centre back bodice opening and matching the side seams but leaving the lining free. Stitch the bodice to the skirt. Turn under 1 cm (½ in) on the lower edge of the lining and slipstitch the folded edge over the skirt/bodice seam.

**9** Make three buttonholes on one side of the bodice back opening and sew three buttons on the other side to correspond.

**10** Wash out the fabric stabiliser. Allow the petticoat to dry, then iron it flat.

*The petticoat*

## Panties

**1** Using the marker pen, trace the pattern from the Pattern Sheet on to the organza or voile. Cut out the pieces.

**2** With right sides facing and raw edges even, sew the centre front and centre back seams.

**3** Neaten the raw edge at the waist, then turn under 1.5 cm (¾ in) to form a casing for the elastic at the waist.

*The panties*

**4** The leg ends are worked in the same stitch as the edge of the petticoat skirt and then cut away. Remember to treat the fabric with the fabric stabiliser before stitching, and with the fray stopper before cutting away the excess fabric on the edges and inside the top row of the scallops. Join the crotch seams.

**5** Working 2 cm (³⁄₄ in) from the leg ends, stitch an encasing stitch to cover the 3 mm (¹⁄₄ in) wide ribbon. It should look as though the ribbon has been threaded through wide entredeux or faggoting. Allow enough ribbon to tie a bow and gather up each leg.

**6** Wash out the fabric stabiliser. Allow the panties to dry, then iron them carefully.

## Dress

**1** Using the marker pen, trace the pattern pieces on to the tulle, then cut them out. Take care to cut the skirt and bodice linings as well. Cut a strip 5 cm x 4 m (2 in x 4¹⁄₂ yd) for the skirt frill and the yoke frill. You will have to join pieces to achieve this length. Tulle is quite expensive so it's a good idea to use every little bit.

Cut another strip 3 cm x 50 cm (1¹⁄₄ in x 20 in) for the neck edge of the yoke.

**2** Join the side seams of the skirt. Cut down the centre back and sew the back placket as for the petticoat.

**3** Using the marker pen, divide and mark the skirt vertically into sixteen equal sections.

**4** Insert a strip of the 2 cm (³⁄₄ in) wide insertion lace over each dividing line, using the following insertion method. First, iron the lace flat, using spray starch to give it extra body. Pin the lace to the right side of the tulle, centred over the dividing lines. Stitch the lace in place, using a small straight stitch and stitching just inside the edges of the lace. On the wrong side, you can cut away the tulle from behind the lace. This is not absolutely necessary as the tulle is very fine and will not show through to the right side.

**5** On either side of each of the sixteen pieces of inserted lace, stitch over a length of 3 mm (¼ in) wide ribbon with an encasing stitch so that it looks like the ribbon has been threaded through faggoting.

**6** Treat the centre of each panel of the skirt with the fabric stabiliser, beginning 3 cm (1¼ in) from the bottom edge and working roughly in the shape of the oval pattern. Allow the tulle to dry, then iron it flat.

**7** Trace the oval pattern on to each skirt panel, making sure each one is centred and begins 3 cm (1¼ in) from the bottom edge of the skirt.

**8** The centre of each oval is embroidered with a pink bunny which was designed on a PC and then transferred to the Pfaff Creative 1475 CD and stitched out automatically. If this is not possible for you, either hand-embroider the bunny in each oval or buy a small lace motif and stitch it in place.

**9** Stitch the edge of each oval with a filled-in scallop which has been reduced (width 6, length 0.25, pattern length 6). Use the needle-down button to pivot as you go around the ovals.

**10** Just inside the straight edge of the scallop, work a small satin stitch to finish off the lace edge.

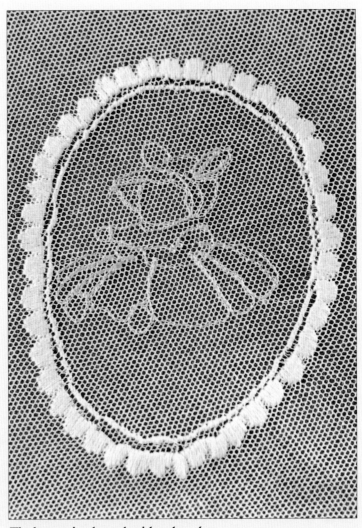

*The bunny in the embroidered oval*

*Figure 2*

*11* Work this same pattern in an oval in the centre of each sleeve and in a circle on the back of the bonnet. All these medallions are worked in the same way.

*12* Join all the pieces to make up the frill for the skirt edge and the yoke. Treat the strip with the fabric stabiliser. Allow the tulle to dry, then iron it flat. Stitch one long side of the frill with the same stitch as on the bottom of the petticoat. Treat the embroidered edge and inside the outer scallops with the fray stopper. Allow the tulle to dry, then cut away the edge of the scallops and the fabric inside the outer scallops, to give a lace cutwork appearance.

*13* Wash the fabric stabiliser out of the skirt and the frill strips.

*14* Slightly gather up the frill strip to fit around the bottom edge of the skirt. Remember to leave enough frill for the bodice yoke.

*15* Join the ends of the frill strip and attach it to the bottom of the skirt.

*16* Treat the centre of the sleeves and the bottom edges of the sleeves with the fabric stabiliser. Work the oval medallion in the centre of each sleeve in the same way as on the skirt. Embroider the lace edges

of the sleeves in the same way as the frill edge. Treat the sleeve edges with the the fray stopper, then cut away the excess fabric as for the skirt.

*17* On either side of the oval medallions in the sleeves, stitch a length of the insertion lace and an enclosed length of the 3 mm (¹/₄ in) wide ribbon as on the skirt.

*18* On the circular front yoke piece, using the marker pen, draw a line 1 cm (¹/₂ in) on either side of the centre front. Attach the insertion lace and enclosed ribbon along these lines, as on the skirt and sleeves.

*19* Join the shoulder seams of the front and back yoke and of the front and back yoke linings.

*20* Treat the small strip of tulle for the neck edge frill with the fabric stabiliser. Work the same type of scallop on one long side of this frill as on the skirt edge but reduced to the smallest width, length and pattern length. You can use the twin needle button to reduce the width even more. Work the same pattern of stitches as on the skirt (two rows of alternating scallops and one row of fine satin stitch). Treat the outside edge with the fray stopper. Allow the tulle to dry, then cut away the excess tulle on the scalloped edge. Wash out the fabric stabiliser. Allow the tulle to dry, then iron it flat.

**21** Gather the strip so that it is 1.5 cm (³/₄ in) wide and long enough to fit the yoke neck edge. Baste the frill around the neck edge with the wrong side of the lace strip facing the right side of the yoke. Pin the yoke lining to the yoke, with right sides together and raw edges even, with the frill in between. Stitch through all thicknesses.

**22** Gather the remaining frill strip to fit the bottom edge of the bodice yoke. Pin and stitch the frill in place.

**23** Join the shoulder seams of the bodice and of the lining. With right sides together, pin the bodice to the bottom edge of the yoke and the bodice lining to the bottom edge of the yoke lining. Stitch. Trim and clip the curves.

**24** Place the complete bodice and lining together, with right sides facing and raw edges even. Stitch them together at the centre back opening edges. Turn the bodice to the right side and press.

**25** Gather the sleeve heads to fit the armholes. Pin the sleeves to the bodice armholes, leaving the lining free. Adjust the gathers to fit and stitch the sleeves in place. Trim the seams and overlock or neaten the seam allowances.

**26** Join the underarm sleeve seams through to the bodice side seams. Trim the seams and press flat. Join the lining side seams.

**27** Stitch a length of the 3 mm (¹/₄ in) wide ribbon 3 cm (1 in) from the bottom edge of each sleeve with the encasing stitch. Pull up the ribbon to gather each sleeve in the same way as the legs of the panties.

**28** Gather the upper edge of the skirt to fit the bodice. Pin the gathered edge to the bodice, matching the centre back opening edges and the side seams. Stitch the skirt to the bodice, leaving the lining free. Press the seam allowance towards the bodice.

**29** On the wrong side, turn under 5 mm (¹/₄ in) on the bodice lining at the sleeve and lower edges. Handstitch in place, covering all the raw edges and seams.

**30** Make three small buttonholes on the centre back opening. Sew on three buttons to correspond.

**31** Wash out the fabric stabiliser and allow the dress to dry, out of the sun. Press. Gather up the sleeves by pulling up the ribbon. Work grub roses in the centre front plain panel of the circular yoke.

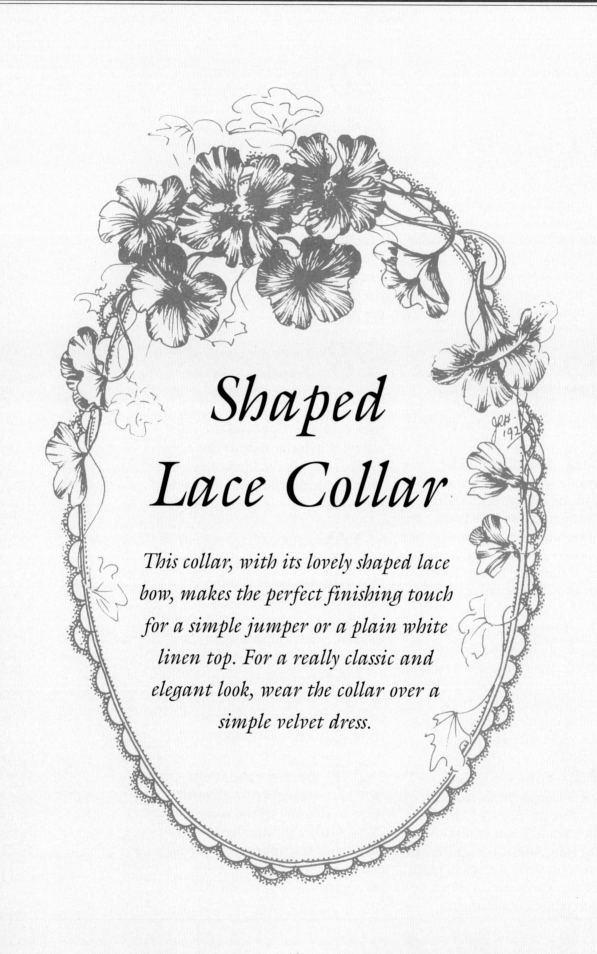

# Shaped Lace Collar

*This collar, with its lovely shaped lace bow, makes the perfect finishing touch for a simple jumper or a plain white linen top. For a really classic and elegant look, wear the collar over a simple velvet dress.*

## MATERIALS

*25 cm (10 in) of cotton net tulle*

*Fabric Stiffener*

*Fray Stoppa*

*one reel of Madeira Tanne white cotton thread*

*narrow batiste bias binding*

*2 m of 1 cm (2¼ yd of ½ in) wide cotton insertion lace*

*one small pearl button*

*ten to twelve small pearl glass beads*

*blue wipe-off fabric marker pen*

*small sharp scissors*

*spray starch*

**The shaped lace bow**

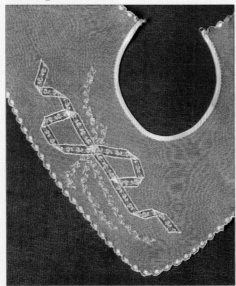

## METHOD

See the collar pattern and the bow shaping design on the Pull out Pattern Sheet.

*1* Using the marker pen, trace the collar pattern on to the piece of tulle. Cut out the pattern piece.

*2* Treat the tulle with fabric stabiliser. Allow the tulle to dry, then iron it carefully so as not to change the shape of the pattern piece.

*3* Trace the bow design on to the tulle, placing it slightly off-centre and towards the left shoulder. Trace in the design lines for the embroidery stitching.

*4* Cut a 60 cm (24 in) length of the cotton insertion lace. Carefully iron it flat, using spray starch to give it extra body. Using the bow pattern on the Pattern Sheet and following the outline of Strip 1 as your guide, lay out the length of insertion lace, turning and mitring the corners as required to achieve the shape.

*5* Pin the lace bow in place on the tulle. On the right side, stitch the bow to the tulle, using a straight stitch and stitching just inside the outside edges of the lace.

*6* Shape and turn a second length of insertion lace, following the outline of Strip 2 on the bow pattern, turning under the raw edges at the beginning and the end as indicated on the pattern. Stitch this length of lace to the tulle in the same way as the first piece.

*7* Using an open flower embroidery stitch, stitch down the five lines as indicated on the pattern.

*8* Embellish the embroidery design by stitching on the small glass beads at appropriate points.

*9* Stitch an open scallop with a heart in the centre around all the outside edges of the collar, except for the neck edge. If you do not have a stitch the same as this, a plain open scallop will do. Stitch.

*10* Treat the outside edges of the collar with the fray stopper. Allow the fabric to dry, then cut away the excess fabric around the outside edge.

*11* Using a herringbone stitch, bind the neck edge with bias binding.

*12* Stitch a small pearl button on one side of the back neck and a small loop buttonhole, made by machine or hand, on the other side.

# *Lacemaking*

The art of lacemaking dates back thousands of years, even as far back as
Ancient Egypt. When the tombs of the Pharoahs were opened and
explored, hair lace was found amongst the Pharoah's treasures.
Beautiful lace has always been prized. At one time, a man's wealth was
judged by the quantity and quality of the lace in his home.
Lace was traditionally made by hand, taking many hours of patience,
practice and perseverance. With the Industrial Revolution came
machine-made lace. Every country developed a reputation for
excellence in a particular type and style of lace, with the best examples
coming out of Europe and England. The most familiar types of
this are Nottingham lace and Brussels lace. Today, it is possible
to design and make your own lace on a computerised
sewing machine; the results are both rewarding and economical.

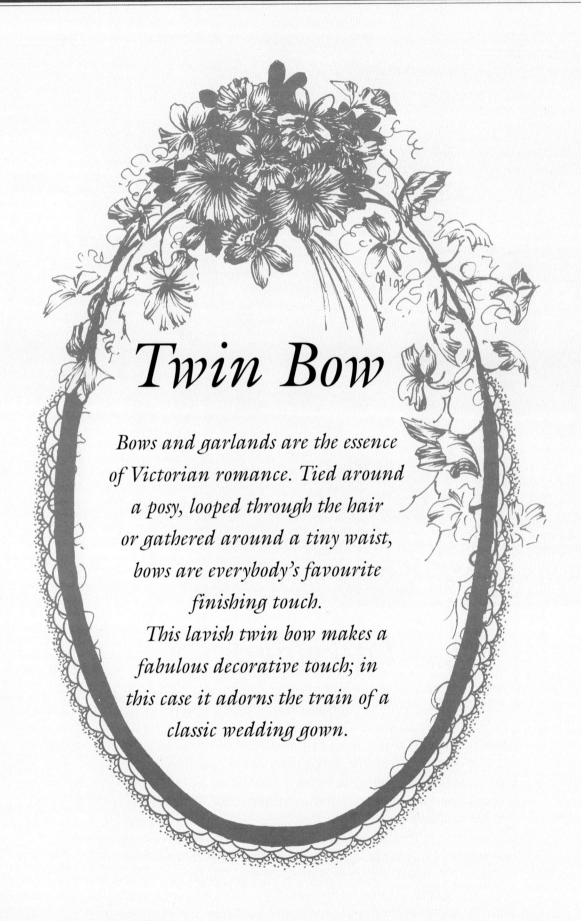

# Twin Bow

*Bows and garlands are the essence
of Victorian romance. Tied around
a posy, looped through the hair
or gathered around a tiny waist,
bows are everybody's favourite
finishing touch.*

*This lavish twin bow makes a
fabulous decorative touch; in
this case it adorns the train of a
classic wedding gown.*

## MATERIALS

*two rectangles of cotton net tulle, each 34 cm x 35 cm (13 1/4 in x 14 in)*

*two reels of Madeira Tanne white cotton thread*

*Fabric Stiffener*

*Fray Stoppa*

*blue wipe-off fabric marker pen*

*small sharp scissors*

*Tear-Away*

**For the antique dye**
*two tea bags*

*two tablespoons of instant coffee*

*two tablespoons of white vinegar*

*two litres (three and a half pints) of boiling water*

## METHOD

See the large twin bow design on the Pull Out Pattern Sheet.

### For the lace panels

*1* Mix the ingredients for the antique dye in a bucket or tub. Immerse both pieces of tulle in the dye. Allow the tulle to dry, then iron it flat.

*2* Treat both pieces of tulle with the fabric stabiliser. Allow the tulle to dry, then iron it flat.

*3* Using the marker pen, draw a guideline down the length of the tulle to give you a straight starting line. After the first row of stitching, use your presser foot as your guide.

*4* Working in straight rows, stitch a variety of machine embroidery stitches that best represent lace stitches along the length of the two rectangles of tulle. Repeat these parallel rows of stitches until all the tulle is covered. Make up two different panels as shown here.

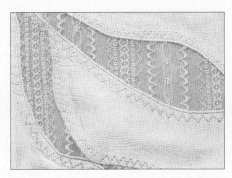

You now have two lace rectangles to use as insertion pieces under the twin bow design.

### To insert the lace

*1* Trace the twin bow from the Pattern Sheet into its exact position on the right side of the fabric, using the marker pen. Note that only half the twin bow pattern is provided; mirror-reverse it to create the other half of the bow.

*2* Work on half the bow at a time. Pin the embroidered tulle rectangle to the back of the fabric under the bow design, placing the pins on the right side of the fabric. On the right side, stitch over all the design lines with a small straight stitch.

*The lace bow*

3   From the front of the fabric and using the small scissors, cut away the fabric between the lines of stitching, allowing you to see the lace work beneath.

4   From the right side of your work, stitch over the straight stitches with an appliqué/satin stitch, taking care to cover the cut away edges as well. Use Tear-Away behind your work if necessary.

5   Using a small open satin stitch scallop, reduced in width, length and pattern length, stitch around the outside edge of the bow and tails, making sure the bottom edge of each scallop meets the appliqué/satin stitch and pivot at points and corners.

6   Working from the back of the fabric, cut away the excess tulle from the outside of the bow design.

NOTE: Position the bow carefully so that the design is not lost in the fabric folds. Using this smaller bow, repeat the motif on the sleeves of the wedding dress as you see here.

*The embroidered bows on the sleeves*

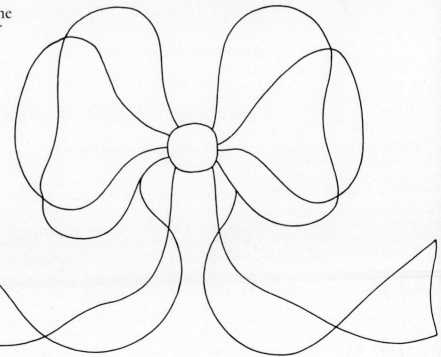

*Bow outline for the sleeves*

# Wedding Dress

*This dress was inspired by my mother's wedding veil. Even though the veil was old and falling apart with age when I first saw it, I remember its beauty and the wonderful silk hand-embroidery that embellished it.*

## MATERIALS

*10 m (11 yd) of cotton net tulle*

*blue wipe-off fabric marker pen*

*Fray Stoppa*

*Fabric Stiffener*

*small sharp scissors*

*eight reels of Madeira Tanne white cotton thread*

*4 m of 3 mm (4½ yd of ¼ in) wide white satin ribbon*

*twelve small pearl buttons*

*1.5 m (1⅔ yd) of strung small pearls*

*various beads, small pearls, glass crystals and shaped pearls*

*10 m (11 yd) of silk ribbon for seam reinforcing*

*15 cm (6 in) square of wadding*

*one Brussels lace butterfly motif*

*120/80 wing needle*

*one hair comb*

*sufficient rosebuds (silk or fresh), wired on to the hair comb to hold the veil*

## METHOD

See the flower embroidery design on the Pull Out Pattern Sheet.

These measurements are approximate and are based on the skirt panel measurements given here and a commercial pattern for the bodice and sleeves.

## Skirt Panels

**1** Cut out three skirt panels from the tulle, each one 75 cm x 1.85 m (30 in x 74 in).

**2** Firstly, design the three skirt pieces. The lace edge should look like pieces of lace joined together as if French sewn. There are seventeen rows of machine-embroidery stitches in the 10 cm (4 in) wide border. (Figure 1)

**3** With the fabric stabiliser, treat the areas that you are going to embroider (in this case, a 10 cm (4 in) border all around the bottom and side edges and a rectangle in the two lower corners of each piece). Allow the tulle to dry, then iron it flat.

**4** Trace the flower design from the Pattern Sheet on to the lower corners of each skirt panel (Figure 2). Embroider the flowers following the stitch key given with the design. Use a small satin stitch for the stem and for the outside edge of the leaves. Stitch a wing needle hem stitch down the stems and around the outside of the centre of the leaves. Stitch two rows of wide satin stitch down the centre of the leaves with hem stitch around the outside shape.

*Figure 1*

Row 2: Reduced filled-in scallop
Row 1: Maxi-scallop
Row 3: As Row 1
Row 4: As Row 1
Row 5: Wing needle hem stitch
Row 6: Fine embroidery stitch
Row 7: As Row 5
Row 8: Satin stitch hearts and circles
Row 9: As Row 5
Row 10: As Row 6
Row 11: As Row 5
Row 12: As Row 2
Row 13: Larger filled-in scallop
Row 14: Satin stitch flowers, leaves and hearts
Row 15: As Row 13
Row 16: As Row 5
Row 17: Partly filled-in scallop

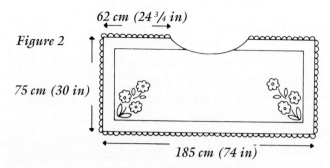

Work around the flowers with a grass appliqué stitch. Before you begin stitching, make sure you know which petals are on top and which ones are underneath so that you can stitch them correctly. On the outside edge of the petals, work a very small filled-in satin stitch scallop. Stitch a wing needle hem stitch where these two rows join.

Stitch the centre of the flowers with a small satin stitch along the 'pinwheel' design lines. Stitch the circular shape with an appliqué/satin stitch, making sure you catch all the ends of the 'pinwheel' lines in the stitching. Around the outside edge of this row, stitch a row of filled-in scallops, pivoting after each scallop so that the scallops follow exactly the circular design line.

**5** Treat the tulle in between each pinwheel line in the centre of each flower with the fray stopper. Allow the tulle to dry, then cut away the tulle so that only the satin stitch lines are left and the result looks like cutwork.

**6** Very loosely measure around your torso at the height of a slightly dropped waist. Divide this measurement into three and scoop out the waist edge for this distance as shown in Figure 2.

**7** The skirt panels are not joined in a traditional seam. Place the scalloped side

*Figure 2*

62 cm (24 ¾ in)

75 cm (30 in)

185 cm (74 in)

edges of two adjacent skirt panels butted together so that the high points of the large scallops are matching. Bar tack them together at this point so that all the scallops match and all the spaces between them match, giving a beautiful lace effect.

*The joined skirt panels*

## Bodice

**1** Using a commercial pattern, cut out a front and two back bodice pieces from the tulle. Allow for a little shrinkage due to the embroidery.

**2** Treat the whole of the bodice pieces with the fabric stabiliser as they will be embroidered all over. Allow the tulle to dry, then iron it flat.

**3** Embroider the bodice with repeating vertical rows of machine-embroidery to look like lace fabric.

*This is not a quick project or one for a beginner. Consider it a long-term project. It takes about four days to embroider each skirt piece. Don't try to rush it.*

Each panel contains the following seven rows of stitches:
Rows 1 and 7: Stitch a filled-in scallop.
Rows 2 and 6: Stitch a wing needle hem stitch.
Rows 3 and 5: Stitch a partly open, partly satin stitch design.
Row 4: Stitch satin stitch hearts and circles.

*Figure 4*

*Rows 1 and 7: Filled-in scallop*
*Rows 2 and 6: Wing needle hem stitch*
*Row 3 and 5: Partly open, partly satin stitch design*
*Row 4: Satin stitch hearts and circles*

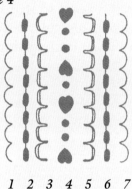

*1  2  3  4  5  6  7*

**4** Join the shoulder seams with French seams, encasing silk ribbon to support the seams.

**5** Stitch a scallop around the neck edge. Treat the outside edge of the scallops with the fray stopper. Allow the tulle to dry, then cut away the excess fabric on the outside edge.

**6** Embroider a small piece of tulle to set behind the V neckline. When the embroidery is completed, sew on beads, pearls and crystals to enhance the embroidery design.

**7** Make twelve looped buttonholes for the back of the bodice and stitch these into place with the facing. Sew on twelve small pearl buttons to correspond.

**8** Join the underarm seams with French seams, again using lengths of silk ribbon to support the seams.

## Sleeves

**1** Cut the sleeves out of tulle, following a commercial pattern. You can also adjust a pattern for simple short sleeves by splitting the sleeve lengthways down the middle and spreading the two halves to add fullness. For the handkerchief hem, cut two 40 cm (16 in) squares and two 30 cm (12 in) squares.

**2** Treat the sleeves with the fabric stabiliser. Allow the tulle to dry, then iron it flat.

**3** Stitch the same embroidered panels as were used on the bodice down the centre of each sleeve, then stitch another panel on each side of the centre one – three panels in all.

**4** Treat 6 cm (2½ in) on all sides of the handkerchief edges of the sleeves with the fabric stabiliser. Stitch these edges with the first three rows of stitching from the edge of the skirt pieces. Treat with the fray stopper, then cut out as for the skirt.

**5** On the centre of each square for the handkerchief frill, mark a circle with the same circumference as the bottom of the sleeves. Cut out the circles. Pin the smaller square on the larger square with the cut-out circles matching.

*Figure 5*

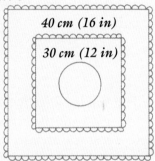

40 cm (16 in)

30 cm (12 in)

**6** Join the underarm sleeve seams with French seams, again using lengths of silk ribbon to support the seams. With right sides together, attach the joined handkerchief frill squares to the ends of each sleeve. Neaten the seam allowance and press towards the sleeve.

Just above the frill and sleeve seam, stitch an encasing stitch over the 3 mm ($\frac{1}{4}$ in) wide ribbon to look as though the ribbon is threaded through faggoting. Pull up the ribbon to gather the bottom edge of the sleeve. Doing it this way allows you to open out the gathers when you wash and iron the dress.

**7** Gather the sleeve heads to fit the armholes. Sew the sleeves into the armholes with lengths of silk ribbon to support the seams.

**8** For the ties, cut two lengths of tulle, each 35 cm x 1 m (14 in x 1$\frac{1}{4}$ yd). Place the two pieces together and cut one end of both ties in a curve. Treat a 5 cm (2 in) border along the long sides and the curved end of each piece with the fabric stabiliser. Work a filled-in scallop stitch around these sides and the curved ends. Treat the edges of the scallops with the fray stopper. Allow the fabric to dry, then cut away the excess fabric on the edges. Wash out the fabric stabiliser, allow the ties to dry and then iron them flat.

## Assembling the garment

**1** Gather up the skirt to fit the bodice. With right sides facing and raw edges even, attach the skirt to the bodice, again sewing in a length of silk ribbon to support the seam.

*A straight strapless slip should be worn under this gown to complete the effect.*

*The wedding dress bodice*

**2** Wash out all the fabric stabiliser. Allow the dress to dry somewhere out of the sun, then iron it flat.

**3** The medallion in the centre front of the skirt (see opposite) is worked in the same way as the motifs on the corners of the skirt panels, except that it is slightly smaller and framed in an oval. Trace the oval and the motif on to a piece of tulle. Place an oval piece of voile on an oval piece of wadding and pin them under the tracing. Embroider the design through all thicknesses, joining the layers together, then bead the medallion with pearls and crystals to highlight the embroidery.

At the centre bottom of the medallion, handstitch the Brussels lace butterfly over the strung beads, looped up and falling down the centre front of the skirt. Attach the straight edges of two scallop-edged ties under the oval medallion, before the medallion is handsewn on to the centre front of the bodice and skirt seam.

## Veil

**1** The veil is basically a triangle with the corners rounded. Treat the area to be embroidered with the fabric stabiliser. Allow the tulle to dry, then iron it flat.

**2** Work the edge with a long filled-in scallop, then stitch a row of 6 mm (1/4 in) wide satin stitch. Between these two rows, work a row of wing needle hem stitch.

**3** Work the floral design in the centre back and in each corner, joining them with half-circles made up of three rows of satin stitch embroidery.

**4** Gather up 40 cm (16 in) in the centre of the long side of the triangle and attach the gathered section to a hair comb. Attach a circle of rosebuds to the comb to hold the veil in place.

*The embroidered and beaded medallion*

*The oval medallion*

# Lace Flowers

All the beauty of a fresh flower is
captured in this creation of net
and lace. Make a lace flower for
the neckline of a special dress or
make a whole bunch for a bridal
bouquet. After the wedding, gather
them into a lovely crystal vase
for your bedside table.

## MATERIALS

*two strips of cotton net tulle, each 8 cm x 70 cm (3 1/4 in x 28 in), for the flowers*

*one strip of cotton net tulle, 10 cm x 20 cm (4 in x 8 in), for the leaves and buds*

*Fabric Stiffener*

*Fray Stoppa*

*blue wipe-off fabric marker pen*

*small sharp scissors*

*one reel of Madeira Tanne cotton thread*

*120 wing needle*

*35 cm (14 in) of 24 gauge florists wire for tying*

*35 cm (14 in) of heavier gauge strong, straight wire for the stem*

*four lengths of covered milliners wire, each 15 cm (6 in)*

*Parafilm*

*stamens*

*small pair of wire cutters (never use scissors to cut wire)*

*craft glue*

## METHOD

See the leaf pattern on the Pull Out Pattern Sheet.

*1* Cut out the strips of tulle and iron them flat. Treat them with the fabric stabiliser, following the manufacturer's instructions.

*2* Stitch the following rows down the entire length of the long strips:
Row 1: On the outside edge, stitch a stepped or plain scallop. Treat the area with the fray stopper, then cut away the excess tulle on the outside edge of the scallops.
Rows 2 and 4: Stitch two rows of hem stitch, using the 120 wing needle, 5 mm (1/4 in) from the inside edge of the scallops and 1.5 cm (3/4 in) apart.
Row 3: Stitch down the centre of the hem stitch rows with an open flower embroidery stitch.

*3* Wash out the fabric stabiliser, allow the tulle to dry, then iron it flat.

*4* To gather the tulle, lengthen your straight stitch to 5 or 6, tighten the upper tension to 7 or 8, and gather the straight edge of the strips of embroidered tulle.

*5* Make a small hook at one end of a length of the heavier gauge wire. Start rolling the gathered tulle around this hook, making the turns larger

and fuller as you work towards the outside of the flower. Using the 24 gauge wire, tie off by wrapping the wire tightly around the bottom (gathered) edge of the flower. Put the flower aside.

*6* To make the leaves, trace two or three leaves on to a smaller piece of stabilised tulle, following the leaf pattern. Place a length of milliners wire on the outside edge of the leaf shape and, using a small satin stitch (width 1.5 to 2.0, length 0.2 to 0.25) stitch over the wire. Position a small piece of wire of a suitable length down the centre of the leaf, leaving about 8 cm (3 1/4 in) of wire at the base of the leaf for attaching it to the stem of the flower. Satin stitch over the wire to form the vein. With the sharp scissors, cut away any excess tulle from the outside edge of the leaves.

*7* Using the Parafilm, wrap the base of the flower (taking care to cover all the wire and fabric) and the wire stem, stretching the Parafilm and turning the flower as you wrap.

*8* Attach the leaves to the flower stem by aligning the leaf stem with the flower stem and wrapping both together as you cover the stem with the Parafilm.

*9* Glue between six and nine stamens into the centre of the flower.

## Bouquet

Calculate how many flowers you will need for your bouquet and work out the quantities of the various materials you will require. Our bouquet has ten large flowers, three medium-sized flowers and three bud-like flowers. The tulle for the bouquet flowers has been dyed using the antique dye on page 18.

You will need 2.5 m of 3 cm (2 ¾ yd x 1¼ in) wide satin ribbon for the loops. If you wish to have long ribbon tails on the bouquet, you will need to allow extra length for this.

## METHOD

*1* Following the instructions for making the flowers, make ten large flowers.

*2* Halve the length of the strips used for making the large flowers and make three medium-sized flowers in the same way.

*3* Halve the length of the strips used for making the medium-sized flowers and make three bud-like flowers in the same way.

*4* Cut the 2.5 m (2 ¾ yd) length of satin ribbon into five equal lengths. With each length, make three loops, approximately 5 cm (2 in) long. Gather the loops together at the base and wire them together, leaving a tail of wire at least 15 cm (6 in) long. Cover the wire

by wrapping it with Parafilm. Make five the same.

*5* Wire the flowers and ribbon loops together to form the bouquet.

If you don't feel confident making the bouquet yourself, make all the flowers and ribbon loops and take them to your local florist to make up for you. Tucking in a little baby's breath creates a lovely soft effect that works very well with the lace flowers.

*These lovely flowers could be used to create a very romantic headdress for a bride and her attendants or for a little girl's first communion.*

*A lace flower and leaf*

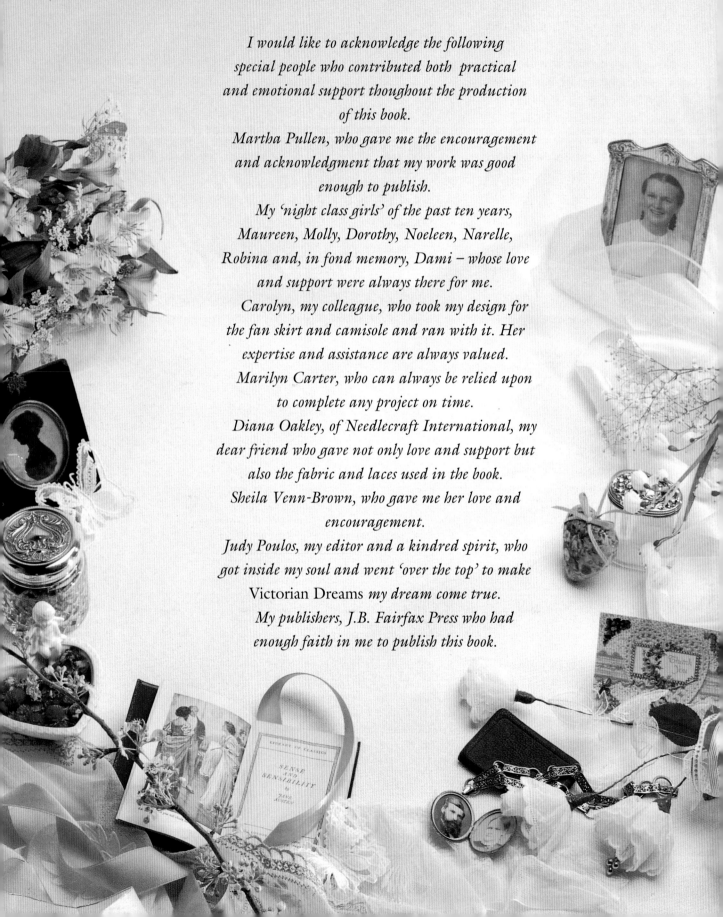

# Acknowledgments

*I would like to acknowledge the following
special people who contributed both practical
and emotional support thoughout the production
of this book.*

*Martha Pullen, who gave me the encouragement
and acknowledgment that my work was good
enough to publish.*

*My 'night class girls' of the past ten years,
Maureen, Molly, Dorothy, Noeleen, Narelle,
Robina and, in fond memory, Dami – whose love
and support were always there for me.*

*Carolyn, my colleague, who took my design for
the fan skirt and camisole and ran with it. Her
expertise and assistance are always valued.*

*Marilyn Carter, who can always be relied upon
to complete any project on time.*

*Diana Oakley, of Needlecraft International, my
dear friend who gave not only love and support but
also the fabric and laces used in the book.*

*Sheila Venn-Brown, who gave me her love and
encouragement.*

*Judy Poulos, my editor and a kindred spirit, who
got inside my soul and went 'over the top' to make
Victorian Dreams my dream come true.*

*My publishers, J.B. Fairfax Press who had
enough faith in me to publish this book.*